Kipling

'If–'
and other poems

Kipling

'If–'
and other poems

Selected and introduced by
DOMINIQUE ENRIGHT

Michael O'Mara Books Limited

This new edition first published in 2016

First published in Great Britain in 2002 by
Michael O'Mara Books Limited
9 Lion Yard, Tremadoc Road
London SW4 7NQ

A CIP catalogue record for this book is available
from the British Library

The text of Kipling's poems as printed here follows
accepted available editions

ISBN 978-1-78243-710-9 in paperback
ISBN 978-1-78243-717-8 in ebook
1 3 5 7 9 10 8 6 4 2

Designed and typeset by Martin Bristow
Printed and bound in Malta by Gutenberg Press

CONTENTS

INTRODUCTION

R UDYARD KIPLING was born in India in 1865, and returned there after schooling in England to take up a career as a journalist. From that simple beginning flowed the poems, short stories and children's books, as well as novels and non-fiction, that would bring him to a peak of popularity, both in Britain and America, that can scarcely be credited today.

To dismiss Kipling as simply an imperialist verse-smith who wrote some engaging children's tales is not only to misjudge both the man and the writer, but also to fail to understand the nature and intention of so much of his poetry. For beyond the occasional bombast, or the expression of ideas belonging now to a past so distant that they have lost all context, lay great warmth of feeling for all humanity, regardless of race or creed.

This pocket-sized selection prints many of Kipling's greatest poems, including extracts from his longer works, in testimony to a writer who possessed, supremely, a precocious gift for rhyme, in which he displays a brilliant ear for language coupled with a pin-sharp use of spare, vivid imagery.

The collection includes: 'Tommy', 'The Way Through the Woods', 'Recessional', 'Boots', 'The Female of the Species', 'Mandalay', 'A Smuggler's Song', 'Gunga Din', 'Danny Deever', 'For All We Have and Are', 'The Absent-Minded Beggar' and extracts from 'McAndrew's Hymn', 'Tomlinson' and 'Epitaphs of the War'.

The Ballad of East and West

(1892)

*Oh, East is East, and West is West, and never the twain shall
    meet,*
*Till Earth and Sky stand presently at God's great Judgment
    Seat;*
*But there is neither East nor West, Border, nor Breed, nor
    Birth,*
*When two strong men stand face to face, though they come
    from the ends of the earth!*

Kamal is out with twenty men to raise the Border-side,
And he has lifted the Colonel's mare that is the Colonel's pride:
He has lifted her out of the stable-door between the dawn and the
    day,
And turned the calkins upon her feet, and ridden her far away.
Then up and spoke the Colonel's son that led a troop of the
    Guides:
'Is there never a man of all my men can say where Kamal hides?'
Then up and spoke Mahommed Khan, the son of the Ressaldar:[1]
'If ye know the track of the morning-mist, ye know where his
    pickets are.
At dusk he harries the Abazai – at dawn he is into Bonair,
But he must go by Fort Bukloh to his own place to fare.

So if ye gallop to Fort Bukloh as fast as a bird can fly,
By the favour of God ye may cut him off ere he win to the
   Tongue of Jagai.
But if he be past the Tongue of Jagai, right swiftly turn ye then,
For the length and the breadth of that grisly plain is sown with
   Kamal's men.
There is rock to the left, and rock to the right, and low lean thorn
   between,
And ye may hear a breech-bolt snick where never a man is seen.'

The Colonel's son has taken a horse, and a raw rough dun was
   he,
With the mouth of a bell and the heart of Hell and the head of
   the gallows-tree.
The Colonel's son to the Fort has won, they bid him stay to eat –
Who rides at the tail of a Border thief, he sits not long at his
   meat.
He's up and away from Fort Bukloh as fast as he can fly,
Till he was aware of his father's mare in the gut of the Tongue of
   Jagai,
Till he was aware of his father's mare with Kamal upon her back,
And when he could spy the white of her eye, he made the pistol
   crack.
He has fired once, he has fired twice, but the whistling ball went
   wide.

'Ye shoot like a soldier,' Kamal said. 'Show now if ye can ride.'
It's up and over the Tongue of Jagai, as blown dust-devils go,
The dun he fled like a stag of ten, but the mare like a barren doe.
The dun he leaned against the bit and slugged his head above,
But the red mare played with the snaffle-bars, as a maiden plays
   with a glove.
There was rock to the left and rock to the right, and low lean
   thorn between,
And thrice he heard a breech-bolt snick tho' never a man was
   seen.
They have ridden the low moon out of the sky, their hoofs drum
   up the dawn,
The dun he went like a wounded bull, but the mare like a new-
   roused fawn.
The dun he fell at a water-course – in a woeful heap fell he,
And Kamal has turned the red mare back, and pulled the rider
   free.
He has knocked the pistol out of his hand – small room was
   there to strive,
''Twas only by favour of mine,' quoth he, 'ye rode so long alive:
There was not a rock for twenty mile, there was not a clump of
   tree,
But covered a man of my own men with his rifle cocked on his
   knee.
If I had raised my bridle-hand, as I have held it low,

The little jackals that flee so fast were feasting all in a row:
If I had bowed my head on my breast, as I have held it high,
The kite that whistles above us now were gorged till she could
    not fly.'
Lightly answered the Colonel's son: 'Do good to bird and beast,
But count who come for the broken meats before thou makest a
    feast.
If there should follow a thousand swords to carry my bones away,
Belike the price of a jackal's meal were more than a thief could
    pay.
They will feed their horse on the standing crop, their men on the
    garnered grain,
The thatch of the byres will serve their fires when all the cattle
    are slain.
But if thou thinkest the price be fair,– thy brethren wait to sup,
The hound is kin to the jackal-spawn,– howl, dog, and call them
    up!
And if thou thinkest the price be high, in steer and gear and
    stack,
Give me my father's mare again, and I'll fight my own way back!'
Kamal has gripped him by the hand and set him upon his feet.
'No talk shall be of dogs,' said he, 'when wolf and grey wolf meet.
May I eat dirt if thou hast hurt of me in deed or breath;
What dam of lances brought thee forth to jest at the dawn with
    Death?'

Lightly answered the Colonel's son: 'I hold by the blood of my
    clan:
Take up the mare for my father's gift – by God, she has carried a
    man!'
The red mare ran to the Colonel's son, and nuzzled against his
    breast;
'We be two strong men,' said Kamal then, 'but she loveth the
    younger best.
So she shall go with a lifter's dower, my turquoise-studded rein,
My 'broidered saddle and saddle-cloth, and silver stirrups twain.'
The Colonel's son a pistol drew and held it muzzle-end,
'Ye have taken the one from a foe,' said he; 'will ye take the mate
    from a friend?'
'A gift for a gift,' said Kamal straight; 'a limb for the risk of a
    limb.
Thy father has sent his son to me, I'll send my son to him!'
With that he whistled his only son, that dropped from a
    mountain-crest –
He trod the ling like a buck in spring, and he looked like a lance
    in rest.
'Now here is thy master,' Kamal said, 'who leads a troop of the
    Guides,
And thou must ride at his left side as shield on shoulder rides.
Till Death or I cut loose the tie, at camp and board and bed,
Thy life is his – thy fate it is to guard him with thy head.

So, thou must eat the White Queen's meat, and all her foes are
   thine,
And thou must harry thy father's hold for the peace of the
   Border-line,
And thou must make a trooper tough and hack thy way to
   power –
Belike they will raise thee to Ressaldar when I am hanged in
   Peshawur!'

They have looked each other between the eyes, and there they
   found no fault,
They have taken the Oath of the Brother-in-Blood on leavened
   bread and salt:
They have taken the Oath of the Brother-in-Blood on fire and
   fresh-cut sod,
On the hilt and the haft of the Khyber knife, and the Wondrous
   Names of God.
The Colonel's son he rides the mare and Kamal's boy the dun,
And two have come back to Fort Bukloh where there went forth
   but one.
And when they drew to the Quarter-Guard, full twenty swords
   flew clear –
There was not a man but carried his feud with the blood of the
   mountaineer.

'Ha' done! ha' done!' said the Colonel's son. 'Put up the steel at
   your sides!
Last night ye had struck at a Border thief – tonight 'tis a man of
   the Guides!'

*Oh, East is East, and West is West, and never the twain shall
   meet,*
*Till Earth and Sky stand presently at God's great Judgment
   Seat;*
*But there is neither East nor West, Border, nor Breed, nor
   Birth,*
*When two strong men stand face to face, though they come
   from the ends of the earth!*

In Partibus

(for *in partibus infidelium* – in countries of the infidels)

The 'buses run to Battersea,
The 'buses run to Bow,
The 'buses run to Westbourne Grove,
And Notting Hill also;
But I am sick of London Town,
From Shepherd's Bush to Bow.

I see the smut upon my cuff,
And feel him on my nose;
I cannot leave my window wide
When gentle Zephyr blows,
Because he brings disgusting things,
And drops 'em on my 'clo'es'.

The sky, a greasy soup-tureen,
Shuts down atop my brow.
Yes, I have sighed for London Town
And I have got it now:
And half of it is fog and filth,
And half is fog and row.

And when I take my nightly prowl,
'Tis passing good to meet
The pious Briton lugging home
His wife and daughter sweet,
Through four packed miles of seething vice,
Thrust out upon the street.

Earth holds no horror like to this
In any land displayed,
From Suez unto Sandy Hook,
From Calais to Port Said;
And 'twas to hide their heathendom
The beastly fog was made.

I cannot tell when dawn is near,
Or when the day is done,
Because I always see the gas
And never see the sun,
And now, methinks, I do not care
A cuss for either one.

But stay, there was an orange, or
An aged egg its yolk;
It might have been a Pears' balloon
Or Barnum's latest joke:
I took it for the sun and wept
To watch it through the smoke.

It's Oh to see the morn ablaze
Above the mango-tope,
When homeward through the dewy cane
The little jackals lope,
And half Bengal heaves into view,
New-washed – with sunlight soap.

It's Oh for one deep whisky-peg
When Christmas winds are blowing,
When all the men you ever knew,
And all you've ceased from knowing,
Are 'entered for the Tournament,
And everything that's going'.

But I consort with long-haired things
In velvet collar-rolls,
Who talk about the Aims of Art,
And 'theories' and 'goals',
And moo and coo with womenfolk
About their blessed souls.

But that they call 'psychology'
Is lack of liver-pill,
And all that blights their tender souls
Is eating till they're ill,
And their chief way of winning goals
Consists of sitting still.

It's Oh to meet an Army man,
Set up, and trimmed and taut,
Who does not spout hashed libraries
Or think the next man's thought,
And walks as though he owned himself,
And hogs his bristles short.

Hear now a voice across the seas
To kin beyond my ken,
If ye have ever filled an hour
With stories from my pen,
For pity's sake send some one here
To bring me news of men!

The 'buses run to Islington,
To Highgate and Soho,
To Hammersmith and Kew
*   therewith,*
And Camberwell also,
But I can only murmur 'Bus!' [1]
From Shepherd's Bush to Bow.

[1] 'Enough!'

Pagett, M.P.

(1886)

The toad beneath the harrow knows
Exactly where each tooth-point goes;
The butterfly upon the road
Preaches contentment to that toad.

Pagett, M.P., was a liar, and a fluent liar therewith –
He spoke of the heat of India as 'The Asian Solar Myth';
Came on a four months' visit, to 'study the East' in November,
And I got him to sign an agreement vowing to stay till September.

March came in with the *koïl*.[1] Pagett was cool and gay,
Called me a 'bloated Brahmin', talked of my 'princely pay'.
March went out with the roses. 'Where is your heat?' said he.
'Coming,' said I to Pagett. 'Skittles!' said Pagett, M.P.

April began with the punkah, coolies, and prickly-heat, –
Pagett was dear to mosquitoes, sandflies found him a treat.
He grew speckled and lumpy – hammered, I grieve to say,
Aryan brothers who fanned him, in an illiberal way.

[1] Indian Bell-bird

May set in with a dust-storm, – Pagett went down with the sun.
All the delights of the season tickled him one by one.
Imprimis – ten days' 'liver' – due to his drinking beer;
Later, a dose of fever – slight, but he called it severe.

Dysent'ry touched him in June, after the *Chota Bursat*[1] –
Lowered his portly person – made him yearn to depart.
He didn't call me a 'Brahmin', or 'bloated', or 'overpaid',
But seemed to think it a wonder that any one ever stayed.

July was a trifle unhealthy, – Pagett was ill with fear.
Called it the 'Cholera Morbus', hinted that life was dear.
He babbled of 'Eastern Exile', and mentioned his home with tears;
But I hadn't seen *my* children for close upon seven years.

We reached a hundred and twenty once in the Court at noon,
(I've mentioned Pagett was portly) Pagett went off in a swoon.
That was an end to the business. Pagett, the perjured, fled
With a practical, working knowledge of 'Solar Myths' in his head.

[1] The early rains

And I laughed as I drove from the station, but the mirth died out
  on my lips
As I thought of the fools like Pagett who write of their 'Eastern
  trips',
And the sneers of the travelled idiots who duly misgovern the
  land,
And I prayed to the Lord to deliver another one into my hand.

Municipal

'Why is my District death-rate low?'
Said Binks of Hezabad.
'Well, drains, and sewage-outfalls are
My own peculiar fad.
I learnt a lesson once. It ran
Thus,' quoth that most veracious man: —

It was an August evening and, in snowy garments clad,
I paid a round of visits in the lines of Hezabad;
When, presently, my Waler saw, and did not like at all,
A Commissariat elephant careering down the Mall.

I couldn't see the driver, and across my mind it rushed
That that Commissariat elephant had suddenly gone *musth*.[1]
I didn't care to meet him, and I couldn't well get down,
So I let the Waler have it, and we headed for the town.

The buggy was a new one and, praise Dykes, it stood the strain,
Till the Waler jumped a bullock just above the City Drain;
And the next that I remember was a hurricane of squeals,
And the creature making toothpicks of my five-foot patent wheels.

---

[1] mad

He seemed to want the owner, so I fled, distraught with fear,
To the Main Drain sewage-outfall while he snorted in my ear –
Reached the four-foot drain-head safely and, in darkness and
   despair,
Felt the brute's proboscis fingering my terror-stiffened hair.

Heard it trumpet on my shoulder – tried to crawl a little higher –
Found the Main Drain sewage-outfall blocked, some eight feet
   up, with mire;
And, for twenty reeking minutes, Sir, my very marrow froze,
While the trunk was feeling blindly for a purchase on my toes!

It missed me by a fraction, but my hair was turning grey
Before they called the drivers up and dragged the brute away.
Then I sought the City Elders, and my words were very plain.
They flushed that four-foot drain-head and – it never choked
   again!

You may hold with surface-drainage, and the sun-for-garbage cure,
Till you've been a periwinkle shrinking coyly up a sewer.
I believe in well-flushed culverts. . . .
   This is why the death-rate's small;
And, if you don't believe me, get *shikarred*[1] yourself. That's all.

---

[1] *shikar*, hunt

Tommy

(1892)

I went into a public-'ouse to get a pint o' beer,
The publican 'e up an' sez, 'We serve no red-coats here.'
The girls be'ind the bar they laughed an' giggled fit to die,
I outs into the street again an' to myself sez I:
   O it's Tommy this, an' Tommy that, an' 'Tommy, go away';
   But it's 'Thank you, Mister Atkins', when the band begins to
     play –
   The band begins to play, my boys, the band begins to play,
   O it's 'Thank you, Mister Atkins', when the band begins to play.

I went into a theatre as sober as could be,
They gave a drunk civilian room, but 'adn't none for me;
They sent me to the gallery or round the music-'alls,
But when it comes to fightin', Lord! they'll shove me in the stalls!
   For it's Tommy this, an' Tommy that, an' 'Tommy, wait
     outside';
   But it's 'Special train for Atkins' when the trooper's on the
     tide –,
   The troopship's on the tide, my boys, the troopship's on the
     tide,
   O it's 'Special train for Atkins' when the trooper's on the tide.

Yes, makin' mock o' uniforms that guard you while you sleep
Is cheaper than them uniforms, an' they're starvation cheap;
An' hustlin' drunken soldiers when they're goin' large a bit
Is five times better business than paradin' in full kit.
　　Then it's Tommy this, an' Tommy that, an' 'Tommy, 'ow's yer
　　　　soul?'
　　But it's 'Thin red line of 'eroes' when the drums begin to roll,
　　The drums begin to roll, my boys, the drums begin to roll,
　　O it's 'Thin red line of 'eroes' when the drums begin to roll.

We aren't no thin red 'eroes, nor we aren't no blackguards too,
But single men in barricks, most remarkable like you;
An' if sometimes our conduck isn't all your fancy paints,
Why, single men in barricks don't grow into plaster saints;
　　While it's Tommy this, an' Tommy that, an' 'Tommy, fall
　　　　be'ind',
　　But it's 'Please to walk in front, sir', when there's trouble in the
　　　　wind,
　　There's trouble in the wind, my boys, there's trouble in the
　　　　wind,
　　O it's 'Please to walk in front, sir', when there's trouble in the
　　　　wind.

You talk o' better food for us, an' schools, an' fires, an' all:
We'll wait for extry rations if you treat us rational.
Don't mess about the cook-room slops, but prove it to our face
The Widow's Uniform is not the soldier-man's disgrace.

For it's Tommy this, an' Tommy that, an' 'Chuck him out, the
brute!'
But it's 'Saviour of 'is country' when the guns begin to shoot;
An' it's Tommy this, an' Tommy that, an' anything you please;
An' Tommy ain't a bloomin' fool – you bet that Tommy sees!

Mandalay

(1892)

By the old Moulmein Pagoda, lookin' lazy at the sea,
There's a Burma girl a-settin', and I know she thinks o' me;
For the wind is in the palm-trees, and the temple-bells they say:
'Come you back, you British soldier; come you back to Mandalay!'
   Come you back to Mandalay,
   Where the old Flotilla lay:
   Can't you 'ear their paddles chunkin' from Rangoon to
     Mandalay?
   On the road to Mandalay,
   Where the flyin'-fishes play,
   An' the dawn comes up like thunder outer China 'crost the Bay!

'Er petticoat was yaller an' 'er little cap was green,
An' 'er name was Supi-yaw-lat – jes' the same as Theebaw's
    Queen,
An' I seed her first a-smokin' of a whackin' white cheroot,
An' a-wastin' Christian kisses on an 'eathen idol's foot:
   Bloomin' idol made o' mud –
   Wot they called the Great Gawd Budd –
   Plucky lot she cared for idols when I kissed 'er where she stud!
   On the road to Mandalay . . .

When the mist was on the rice-fields an' the sun was droppin'
    slow,
She'd git 'er little banjo an' she'd sing '*Kulla-lo-lo!*'
With 'er arm upon my shoulder an' 'er cheek agin' my cheek
We useter watch the steamers an' the *hathis* pilin' teak.
   Elephints a-pilin' teak
   In the sludgy, squdgy creek,
   Where the silence 'ung that 'eavy you was 'arf afraid to speak!
   On the road to Mandalay . . .

But that's all shove be'ind me – long ago an' fur away,
An' there ain't no 'buses runnin' from the Bank to Mandalay;
An' I'm learnin' 'ere in London what the ten-year soldier tells:
'If you've 'eard the East a-callin', you won't never 'eed naught
    else.'
   No! you won't 'eed nothin' else
   But them spicy garlic smells,
   An' the sunshine an' the palm-trees an' the tinkly temple-bells;
   On the road to Mandalay . . .

I am sick o' wastin' leather on these gritty pavin'-stones,
An' the blasted English drizzle wakes the fever in my bones;
Tho' I walks with fifty 'ousemaids outer Chelsea to the Strand,
An' they talks a lot o' lovin', but wot do they understand?
     Beefy face an' grubby 'and –
     Law! wot do they understand?
     I've a neater, sweeter maiden in a cleaner, greener land!
     On the road to Mandalay . . .

Ship me somewheres east of Suez, where the best is like the worst,
Where there aren't no Ten Commandments an' a man can raise
     a thirst;
For the temple-bells are callin', an' it's there that I would be –
By the old Moulmein Pagoda, looking lazy at the sea;
     On the road to Mandalay,
     Where the old Flotilla lay,
     With our sick beneath the awnings when we went to Mandalay!
     On the road to Mandalay,
     Where the flyin'-fishes play,
     An' the dawn comes up like thunder outer China 'crost the Bay!

A Code of Morals

Lest you should think this story true
I merely mention I
Evolved it lately. 'Tis a most
Unmitigated misstatement.

Now Jones had left his new-wed bride to keep his house in order,
And hied away to the Hurrum Hills above the Afghan border,
To sit on a rock with a heliograph; but ere he left he taught
His wife the working of the Code that sets the miles at naught.

And Love had made him very sage, as Nature made her fair;
So Cupid and Apollo linked, *per* heliograph, the pair.
At dawn, across the Hurrum Hills, he flashed her counsel wise –
At e'en, the dying sunset bore her husband's homilies.

He warned her 'gainst seductive youths in scarlet clad and gold,
As much as 'gainst the blandishments paternal of the old;
But kept his gravest warnings for (hereby the ditty hangs)
That snowy-haired Lothario, Lieutenant-General Bangs.

'Twas General Bangs, with Aide and Staff, that tittupped on the
   way,
When they beheld a heliograph tempestuously at play.
They thought of Border risings, and of stations sacked and
   burnt –
So stopped to take the message down – and this is what they
   learnt –

'Dash dot dot, dot, dot dash, dot dash dot' twice. The General
   swore.
'Was ever General Officer addressed as "dear" before?
"My Love," i' faith! "My Duck," Gadzooks! "My darling popsy-
   wop!"
Spirit of great Lord Wolseley, *who* is on that mountaintop?'

The artless Aide-de-camp was mute; the gilded Staff were still,
As, dumb with pent-up mirth, they booked that message from the
   hill;
For clear as summer lightning-flare, the husband's warning ran: –
'Don't dance or ride with General Bangs – a most immoral man.'

(At dawn, across the Hurrum Hills, he flashed her counsel wise –
But, howsoever Love be blind, the world at large hath eyes.)
With damnatory dot and dash he heliographed his wife
Some interesting details of the General's private life.

The artless Aide-de-camp was mute, the shining Staff were still,
And red and ever redder grew the General's shaven gill.
And this is what he said at last (his feelings matter not): –
'I think we've tapped a private line. Hi! Threes about there! Trot!'

All honour unto Bangs, for ne'er did Jones thereafter know
By word or act official who read off that helio.
But the tale is on the Frontier, and from Michni to Mool*tan*
They know the worthy General as 'that most immoral man.'

Gunga Din
(1892)

You may talk o' gin and beer
When you're quartered safe out 'ere,
An' you're sent to penny-fights an' Aldershot it;
But when it comes to slaughter
You will do your work on water,
An' you'll lick the bloomin' boots of 'im that's got it.
Now in Injia's sunny clime,
Where I used to spend my time
A-servin' of 'Er Majesty the Queen,
Of all them blackfaced crew
The finest man I knew
Was our regimental bhisti, Gunga Din.
 He was 'Din! Din! Din!
 You limpin' lump o' brick-dust, Gunga Din!
 Hi! slippy *hitherao*!
 Water, get it! *Panee lao*![1]
 You squidgy-nosed old idol, Gunga Din.'

[1] Bring water quick

The uniform 'e wore
Was nothin' much before,
An' rather less than 'arf o' that be'ind,
For a piece o' twisty rag
An' a goatskin water-bag
Was all the field-equipment 'e could find.
When the sweatin' troop-train lay
In a sidin' through the day,
Where the 'eat would make your bloomin' eyebrows crawl,
We shouted 'Harry By!' [2]
Till our throats were bricky-dry,
Then we wopped 'im 'cause 'e couldn't serve us all.

 It was 'Din! Din! Din!
 You 'eathen, where the mischief 'ave you been?
 You put some *juldee* [3] in it
 Or I'll *marrow* [4] you this minute
 If you don't fill up my helmet, Gunga Din!'

[2] O brother

[3] be quick

[4] hit you

'E would dot an' carry one
Till the longest day was done;
An' 'e didn't seem to know the use o' fear.
If we charged or broke or cut,
You could bet your bloomin' nut,
'E'd be waitin' fifty paces right flank rear.
With 'is *mussick*⁵ on 'is back,
'E would skip with our attack,
An' watch us till the bugles made 'Retire',
An' for all 'is dirty 'ide
'E was white, clear white, inside
When 'e went to tend the wounded under fire!
   It was 'Din! Din! Din!'
   With the bullets kickin' dust-spots on the green.
   When the cartridges ran out,
   You could hear the front-files shout,
   'Hi! ammunition-mules an' Gunga Din!'

⁵ water skin

I shan't forgit the night
When I dropped be'ind the fight
With a bullet where my belt-plate should 'a' been.
I was chokin' mad with thirst,
An' the man that spied me first
Was our good old grinnin', gruntin' Gunga Din.
'E lifted up my 'ead,
An' he plugged me where I bled,
An' 'e guv me 'arf-a-pint o' water green:
It was crawlin' and it stunk,
But of all the drinks I've drunk,
I'm gratefullest to one from Gunga Din.
   It was 'Din! Din! Din!
   'Ere's a beggar with a bullet through 'is spleen;
   'E's chawin' up the ground,
   An' 'e's kickin' all around:
   For Gawd's sake git the water, Gunga Din!'

'E carried me away
To where a dooli lay,
An' a bullet come an' drilled the beggar clean.
'E put me safe inside,
An' just before 'e died,
'I 'ope you liked your drink', sez Gunga Din.
So I'll meet 'im later on
At the place where 'e is gone –
Where it's always double drill and no canteen;
'E'll be squattin' on the coals
Givin' drink to poor damned souls,
An' I'll get a swig in hell from Gunga Din!
  Yes, Din! Din! Din!
  You Lazarushian-leather Gunga Din!
  Though I've belted you and flayed you,
  By the livin' Gawd that made you,
  You're a better man than I am, Gunga Din!

Danny Deever

(1892)

'What are the bugles blowin' for?' said Files-on-Parade.
'To turn you out, to turn you out,' the Colour-Sergeant said.
'What makes you look so white, so white?' said Files-on-Parade.
'I'm dreadin' what I've got to watch,' the Colour-Sergeant said.
  For they're hangin' Danny Deever, you can hear the Dead
      March play,
  The Regiment's in 'ollow square – they're hangin' him today;
  They've taken of his buttons off an' cut his stripes away,
  An' they're hangin' Danny Deever in the mornin'.

'What makes the rear-rank breathe so 'ard?' said Files-on-Parade.
'It's bitter cold, it's bitter cold,' the Colour-Sergeant said.
'What makes that front-rank man fall down?' said Files-on-
    Parade.
'A touch o' sun, a touch o' sun,' the Colour-Sergeant said.
  They are hangin' Danny Deever, they are marchin' of 'im
      round,
  They 'ave 'alted Danny Deever by 'is coffin on the ground;
  An' 'e'll swing in 'arf a minute for a sneakin' shootin' hound –
  O they're hangin' Danny Deever in the mornin'!

''Is cot was right-'and cot to mine,' said Files-on-Parade.
'E's sleepin' out an' far tonight,' the Colour-Sergeant said.
'I've drunk 'is beer a score o' times,'said Files-on-Parade.
'E's drinkin' bitter beer alone,' the Colour-Sergeant said.
  They are hangin' Danny Deever, you must mark 'im to 'is
     place,
  For 'e shot a comrade sleepin' – you must look 'im in the face;
  Nine 'undred of 'is county an' the Regiment's disgrace,
  While they're hangin' Danny Deever in the mornin'.

'What's that so black agin' the sun?' said Files-on-Parade.
'It's Danny fightin' 'ard for life,' the Colour-Sergeant said.
'What's that that whimpers over'ead?' said Files-on-Parade.
'It's Danny's soul that's passin' now,' the Colour-Sergeant said.
  For they're done with Danny Deever, you can 'ear the quickstep
     play,
  The Regiment's in column, an' they're marchin' us away;
  Ho! the young recruits are shakin', an' they'll want their beer
     today,
  After hangin' Danny Deever in the mornin'!

The Last Department

Twelve hundred million men are spread
About this Earth, and I and You
Wonder, when You and I are dead,
'What will those luckless millions do?'

'None whole or clean,' we cry, 'or free from stain
Of favour.' Wait awhile, till we attain
The Last Department where nor fraud nor fools,
Nor grade nor greed, shall trouble us again.

Fear, Favour, or Affection – what are these
To the grim Head who claims our services?
I never knew a wife or interest yet
Delay that *pukka* step, miscalled 'decease';

When leave, long overdue, none can deny;
When idleness of all Eternity
Becomes our furlough, and the marigold
Our thriftless, bullion-minting Treasury

Transferred to the Eternal Settlement,
Each in his strait, wood-scantled office pent,
No longer Brown reverses Smith's appeals,
Or Jones records his Minute of Dissent.

And One, long since a pillar of the Court,
As mud between the beams thereof is wrought;
And One who wrote on phosphates for the crops
Is subject-matter of his own Report.

These be the glorious ends whereto we pass –
Let Him who Is, go call on Him who Was;
And He shall see the *mallie*[1] steals the slab
For curry-grinder, and for goats the grass.

A breath of wind, a Border bullet's flight,
A draught of water, or a horse's fright –
The droning of the fat *Sheristadar*[2]
Ceases, the punkah stops, and falls the night

For You or Me. Do those who live decline
The step that offers, or their work resign?
Trust me, To-day's Most Indispensables,
Five hundred men can take your place or mine.

[1] cemetery gardener   [2] Clerk of the Court

From **Tomlinson**
(1891)

Now Tomlinson gave up the ghost in his house in Berkeley Square,
And a Spirit came to his bedside and gripped him by the hair –
A Spirit gripped him by the hair and carried him far away,
Till he heard as the roar of a rain-fed ford the roar of the Milky
    Way:
Till he heard the roar of the Milky Way die down and drone and
    cease,
And they came to the Gate within the Wall where Peter holds the
    keys.
'Stand up, stand up now, Tomlinson, and answer loud and high
The good that ye did for the sake of men or ever ye came to die –
The good that ye did for the sake of men in little Earth so lone!'
And the naked soul of Tomlinson grew white as a rain-washed
    bone.
'O I have a friend on Earth,' he said, 'that was my priest and
    guide,
And well would he answer all for me if he were by my side.'
– 'For that ye strove in neighbour-love it shall be written fair,
But now ye wait at Heaven's Gate and not in Berkeley Square:
Though we called your friend from his bed this night, he could
    not speak for you,
For the race is run by one and one and never by two and two.'

[. . .] 'O this I have read in a book,' he said, 'and that was told to
     me,
And this I have thought that another man thought of a Prince in
     Muscovy.'
[. . .] 'Ye have read, ye have felt, ye have guessed, good lack! Ye
     have hampered Heaven's Gate;
There's little room between the stars in idleness to prate!
For none may reach by hired speech of neighbour, priest, and kin
Through borrowed deed to God's good meed that lies so fair within;
Get hence, get hence to the Lord of Wrong, for the doom has yet
     to run,
And . . . the faith that ye share with Berkeley Square uphold you,
     Tomlinson!'

The Spirit gripped him by the hair, and sun by sun they fell
Till they came to the belt of Naughty Stars that rim the mouth of
     Hell:
[. . .] The Wind that blows between the Worlds, it nipped him to
     the bone,
And he yearned to the flare of Hell-gate there as the light of his
     own hearth-stone.
The Devil he sat behind the bars, where the desperate legions
     drew,
But he caught the hasting Tomlinson and would not let him
     through.

[45]

[. . .] 'Sit down, sit down upon the slag, and answer loud and
   high
The harm that ye did to the Sons of Men or ever you came to
   die.'
[. . .] 'O I had a love on earth,' said he, 'that kissed me to my
   fall;
And if ye would call my love to me I know she would answer
   all.'
– 'All that ye did in love forbid it shall be written fair,
But now ye wait at Hell-Mouth Gate and not in Berkeley Square:
Though we whistled your love from her bed tonight, I trow she
   would not run,
For the sin ye do by two and two ye must pay for one by one!'
[. . .] 'Nay, this I ha' heard,' quo' Tomlinson, 'and this was
   noised abroad,
And this I ha' got from a Belgian book on the word of a dead
   French lord.'
– 'Ye ha' heard, ye ha' read, ye ha' got, good lack! and the tale
   begins afresh –
Have ye sinned one sin for the pride o' the eye or the sinful lust
   of the flesh?'
Then Tomlinson he gripped the bars and yammered, 'Let me
   in –
For I mind that I borrowed my neighbour's wife to sin the
   deadly sin.'

The Devil he grinned behind the bars, and banked the fires
   high:
'Did ye read of that sin in a book?' said he; and Tomlinson said,
   'Ay!'
The Devil he blew upon his nails, and the little devils ran,
And he said: 'Go husk this whimpering thief that comes in the
   guise of a man:
Winnow him out 'twixt star and star, and sieve his proper worth:
There's sore decline in Adam's line if this be spawn of earth.'
[. . .] And back they came with the tattered Thing, as children
   after play,
And they said: 'The soul that he got from God he has bartered
   clean away.'
[. . .] The Devil he looked at the mangled Soul that prayed to
   feel the flame,
And he thought of Holy Charity, but he thought of his own good
   name: –
'Now ye could haste my coal to waste, and sit ye down to fry:
Did ye think of that theft for yourself?' said he; and Tomlinson
   said, 'Ay!'
The Devil he blew an outward breath, for his heart was free from
   care: –
'Ye have scarce the soul of a louse,' he said, 'but the roots of sin
   are there,
And for that sin should ye come in were I the lord alone.

[47]

But sinful pride has rule inside – ay, mightier than my own.
Honour and Wit, fore-damned they sit, to each his Priest and
    Whore:
Nay, scarce I dare myself go there, and you they'd torture sore.
Ye are neither spirit nor spirk,' he said; 'ye are neither book nor
    brute –
Go, get ye back to the flesh again for the sake of Man's repute.
I'm all o'er-sib to Adam's breed that I should mock your pain,
But look that ye win to worthier sin ere ye come back again.
Get hence, the hearse is at your door – the grim black stallions
    wait –
They bear your clay to place to-day. Speed, lest ye come too late!
Go back to Earth with a lip unsealed – go back with an open eye,
And carry my word to the Sons of Men or ever ye come to die:
That the sin they do by two and two they must pay for one by
    one,
And . . . the God that you took from a printed book be with you,
    Tomlinson!'

Road Song of the Bandar-Log

('Kaa's Hunting', *The Jungle Book*, 1894)

Here we go in a flung festoon,
Half-way up to the jealous moon!
Don't you envy our pranceful bands?
Don't you wish you had extra hands?
Wouldn't you like if your tails were – *so* –
Curved in the shape of a Cupid's bow?
  Now you're angry, but – never mind,
  Brother, thy tail hangs down behind!

Here we sit in a branchy row,
Thinking of beautiful things we know;
Dreaming of deeds that we mean to do,
All complete, in a minute or two –
Something noble and grand and good,
Won by merely wishing we could.
  Now we're going to – never mind,
  Brother, thy tail hangs down behind!

All the talk we ever have heard
Uttered by bat or beast or bird –
Hide or fin or scale or feather –
Jabber it quickly and all together!
Excellent! Wonderful! Once again!
Now we are talking just like men!
    Let's pretend we are . . . never mind,
    Brother, thy tail hangs down behind!
    This is the way of the monkey-kind.

Then join our leaping lines that scumfish through the pines,
That rocket by where, light and high, the wild-grape swings.
By the rubbish in our wake, and the noble noise we make,
Be sure – be sure, we're going to do some splendid things!

I Keep Six Honest Serving-men

('The Elephant's Child', *Just So Stories*, 1902)

I keep six honest serving-men
(They taught me all I knew);
Their names are What and Why and When
And How and Where and Who.
I send them over land and sea,
I send them east and west;
But after they have worked for me,
I give them all a rest.

I let them rest from nine till five,
For I am busy then,
As well as breakfast, lunch, and tea,
For they are hungry men.
But different folk have different views;
I know a person small –
She keeps ten million serving-men,
Who get no rest at all!

She sends 'em abroad on her own affairs,
From the second she opens her eyes –
One million Hows, two million Wheres,
And seven million Whys!

Parade-Song of the Camp-Animals

('Her Majesty's Servants', *The Jungle Book*, 1894)

ELEPHANTS OF THE GUN-TEAMS

We lent to Alexander the strength of Hercules,
The wisdom of our foreheads, the cunning of our knees.
We bowed our necks to service – they ne'er were loosed again, –
Make way there, way for the ten-foot teams
Of the Forty-Pounder train!

GUN-BULLOCKS

Those heroes in their harnesses avoid a cannon-ball,
And what they know of powder upsets them one and all;
Then we come into action and tug the guns again, –
Make way there, way for the twenty yoke
Of the Forty-Pounder train!

CAVALRY HORSES

By the brand on my withers, the finest of tunes
Is played by the Lancers, Hussars, and Dragoons,
And it's sweeter than 'Stables' or 'Water' to me,
The Cavalry Canter of 'Bonnie Dundee'!

Then feed us and break us and handle and groom,
And give us good riders and plenty of room,
And launch us in column of squadron and see
The Way of the War-horse to 'Bonnie Dundee'!

Screw-Gun Mules

As me and my companions were scrambling up a hill,
The path was lost in rolling stones, but we went forward still;
For we can wriggle and climb, my lads, and turn up everywhere,
And it's our delight on a mountain height, with a leg or two to
    spare!

Good luck to every sergeant, then, that lets us pick our road!
Bad luck to all the driver-men that cannot pack a load!
For we can wriggle and climb, my lads, and turn up everywhere,
And it's our delight on a mountain height, with a leg or two to
    spare!

COMMISSARIAT CAMELS

We haven't a camelty tune of our own
To help us trollop along,
But every neck is a hair-trombone
(*Rtt-ta-ta-ta!* is a hair-trombone!)
And this is our marching-song:
Can't! Don't! Shan't! Won't!
Pass it along the line!
Somebody's pack has slid from his back,
'Wish it were only mine!
Somebody's load has tipped off in the road –
Cheer for a halt and a row!
Urrr! Yarrh! Grr! Arrh!
Somebody's catching it now!

Children of the Camp are we,
Serving each in his degree;
Children of the yoke and goad,
Pack and harness, pad and load.
See our line across the plain,
Like a heel-rope bent again,
Reaching, writhing, rolling far,
Sweeping all away to war!
While the men that walk beside,
Dusty, silent, heavy-eyed,
Cannot tell why we or they
March and suffer day by day.
  Children of the Camp are we,
  Serving each in his degree;
  Children of the yoke and goad,
  Pack and harness, pad and load!

Mowgli's Song Against People

('Letting in the Jungle', *The Second Jungle Book*,1895)

I will let loose against you the fleet-footed vines –
I will call in the Jungle to stamp out your lines!
   The roofs shall fade before it,
     The house-beams shall fall;
And the *Karela*,[1] the bitter *Karela*,
     Shall cover it all!

In the gates of these your councils my people shall sing.
In the doors of these your garners the Bat-folk shall cling;
   And the snake shall be your watchman,
     By a hearthstone unswept;
For the *Karela*, the bitter *Karela*,
     Shall fruit where ye slept!

Ye shall not see my strikers; ye shall hear them and guess.
By night, before the moon-rise, I will send for my cess,
   And the wolf shall be your herdsman
     By a landmark removed;
For the *Karela*, the bitter *Karela*,
     Shall seed where ye loved!

I will reap your fields before you at the hands of a host.
Ye shall glean behind my reapers for the bread that is lost;
   And the deer shall be your oxen
     On a headland untilled:
  For the *Karela*, the bitter *Karela*,
     Shall leaf where ye build!

I have untied against you the club-footed vines –
I have sent in the Jungle to swamp out your lines!
   The trees – the trees are on you!
    The house-beams shall fall;
  And the *Karela*, the bitter *Karela*,
     Shall cover you all!

---

[1] a kind of wild melon

From **McAndrew's Hymn**
(1893)

Lord, Thou hast made this world below the shadow of a dream,
An', taught by time, I tak' it so – exceptin' always Steam.
From coupler-flange to spindle-guide I see Thy Hand, O God –
Predestination in the stride o' yon connectin'-rod.
John Calvin might ha' forged the same – enorrmous, certain,
   slow –
Ay, wrought it in the furnace-flame – *my* 'Institutio'.
I cannot get my sleep to-night; old bones are hard to please;
I'll stand the middle watch up here – alone wi' God an' these
My engines, after ninety days o' race an' rack an' strain
Through all the seas of all Thy world, slam-bangin' home again.
Slam-bang too much – they knock a wee – the crosshead-gibs
   are loose,
But thirty thousand mile o' sea has gied them fair excuse […]
… Not but that they're ceevil on the Board. Ye'll hear Sir
   Kenneth say:
'Good morrn, McAndrew! Back again? An' how's your bilge
   today?'
Miscallin' technicalities but handin' me my chair
To drink Madeira wi' three Earls – the auld Fleet Engineer
That started as a boiler-whelp – when steam and he were low.
I mind the time we used to serve a broken pipe wi' tow!

[58]

Ten pound was all the pressure then – Eh! Eh! – a man wad
　　drive;
An' here, our workin' gauges give one hunder sixty-five!
We're creepin' on wi' each new rig – less weight an' larger
　　power;
There'll be the loco-boiler next an' thirty mile an hour!
Thirty an' more. What I ha' seen since ocean-steam began
Leaves me na doot for the machine: but what about the man?
The man that counts, wi' all his runs, one million mile o' sea:
Four time the span from earth to moon . . . How far, O Lord,
　　from Thee
That wast beside him night an' day? Ye mind my first typhoon?
It scoughed the skipper on his way to jock wi' the saloon.
Three feet were on the stokehold-floor – just slappin' to an' fro –
An' cast me on a furnace-door. I have the marks to show.
Marks! I ha' marks o' more than burns – deep in my soul an'
　　black,
An' times like this, when things go smooth, my wickudness
　　comes back.
The sins o' four an' forty years, all up an' down the seas.
Clack an' repeat like valves half-fed . . . Forgie's our trespasses!
　　[. . .]
. . . Till, off Sambawa Head, Ye mind, I heard a land-breeze ca',
Milk-warm wi' breath o' spice an' bloom: 'McAndrew, come
　　awa'!'

Firm, clear an' low – no haste, no hate – the ghostly whisper
  went,
Just statin' eevidential facts beyon' all argument:
'Your mither's God's a graspin' deil, the shadow o' yoursel',
Got out o' books by meenisters clean daft on Heaven an' Hell.
They mak' him in the Broomielaw, o' Glasgie cold an' dirt,
A jealous, pridefu' fetich, lad, that's only strong to hurt.
Ye'll not go back to Him again an' kiss His red-hot rod,
But come wi' Us' (Now, who were *They*?) 'an' know the Leevin'
  God,
That does not kipper souls for sport or break a life in jest,
But swells the ripenin' coconuts an' ripes the woman's breast.'
An' there it stopped – cut off – no more – that quiet, certain
  voice –
For me, six months o' twenty-four, to leave or take at choice.
'Twas on me like a thunderclap – it racked me through an'
  through –
Temptation past the show o' speech, unnameable an' new –
The Sin against the Holy Ghost? . . . An' under all, our screw.

That storm blew by but left behind her anchor-shiftin' swell.
Thou knowest all my heart an' mind, Thou knowest, Lord, I fell –
Third on the *Mary Gloster* then, and first that night in Hell!
Yet was Thy Hand beneath my head, about my feet Thy Care –
Fra' Deli clear to Torres Strait, the trial o' despair,

But when we touched the Barrier Reef Thy answer to my
    prayer! . . .
We dared na run that sea by night but lay an' held our fire,
An' I was drowsin' on the hatch – sick – sick wi' doubt an' tire:
'Better the sight of eyes that see than wanderin' o' desire!'
Ye mind that word? Clear as gongs – again, an' once again,
When rippin' down through coral-trash ran out our moorin'-
    chain:
An', by Thy Grace, I had the light to see my duty plain.
Light on the engine-room – no more – bright as our carbons
    burn.
I've lost it since a thousand times, but never past return!

Obsairve! Per annum we'll have here two thousand souls
    aboard –
Think not I dare to justify myself before the Lord,
But – average fifteen hunder souls safe-born fra' port to port –
I *am* o' service to my kind. Ye wadna blame the thought?
Maybe they steam from Grace to Wrath – to sin by folly led –
It isna mine to judge their path – their lives are on my head.
Mine at the last – when all is done it all comes back to me,
The fault that leaves six thousand ton a log upon the sea.[…]
… Yon's strain, hard strain, o' head an' hand, for though Thy
    Power brings
All skill to naught, Ye'll understand a man must think o' things.

Then, at the last, we'll get to port an' hoist their baggage clear –
The passengers, wi' gloves an' canes – an' this is what I'll hear:
'Well, thank ye for a pleasant voyage. The tender's comin' now.'
While I go testin' follower-bolts an' watch the skipper bow.
They've words for every one but me – shake hands wi' half the crew,
Except the dour Scots engineer, the man they never knew.
An' yet I like the wark for all we've dam'-few pickin's here –
No pension, an' the most we'll earn's four hunder pound a year.
   [...]
. . . Below there! Oiler! What's your wark? Ye find it runnin' hard?
Ye needn't swill the cup wi' oil – this isn't the Cunard!
Ye thought? Ye are not paid to think. Go, sweat that off again!
Tck! Tck! It's deeficult to sweer nor tak' The Name in vain!
Men, ay an' women, call me stern. Wi' these to oversee,
Ye'll note I've little time to burn on social repartee.
The bairns see what their elders miss; they'll hunt me to an' fro,
Till for the sake of – well, a kiss – I tak' 'em down below.
That minds me of our Viscount loon – Sir Kenneth's kin – the chap
Wi' Russia-leather tennis-shoon an' spar-decked yachtin'-cap.
I showed him round last week, o'er all – an' at the last says he:
'Mister McAndrew, don't you think steam spoils romance at sea?'

Damned ijjit! I'd been doon that morn to see what ailed the
   throws,
Manholin', on my back – the cranks three inches off my nose.
Romance! Those first-class passengers they like it very well,
Printed an' bound in little books; but why don't poets tell?
I'm sick of all their quirks an' turns – the loves an' doves they
   dream –
Lord, send a man like Robbie Burns to sing the Song o' Steam!
To match wi' Scotia's noblest speech yon orchestra sublime
Whaurto – uplifted like the Just – the tail-rods mark the time.
The crank-throws give the double-bass, the feed-pump sobs an'
   heaves,
An' now the main eccentrics start their quarrel on the sheaves:
Her time, her own appointed time, the rocking link-head bides,
Till – hear that note? – the rod's return whings glimmerin'
   through the guides.
They're all awa'! True beat, full power, the clangin' chorus goes
Clear to the tunnel where they sit, my purrin' dynamoes.
Interdependence absolute, foreseen, ordained, decreed,
To work, Ye'll note, at ony tilt an' every rate o' speed.
Fra' skylight-lift to furnace-bars, backed, bolted, braced an'
   stayed,
An' singin' like the Mornin' Stars for joy that they are made;
While, out o' touch o' vanity, the sweatin' thrust-block says:

'Not unto us the praise, or man – not unto us the praise!' [...]
... Uplift am I? When first in store the new-made beasties stood,
Were Ye cast down that breathed the Word declarin' all things
    good?
Not so! O' that warld-liftin' joy no after-fall could vex,
Ye've left a glimmer still to cheer the Man – the Arrtifex!
That holds, in spite o' knock and scale, o' friction, waste an' slip,
An' by that light – now, mark my word – we'll build the Perfect
    Ship.
I'll never last to judge her lines, or take her curve – not I.
But I ha' lived an' I ha' worked. Be thanks to Thee, Most High!
An' I ha' done what I ha' done – judge Thou if ill or well –
Always Thy Grace preventin' me ...
    Losh! Yon's the 'Stand-by' bell.
Pilot so soon? His flare it is. The mornin'-watch is set.
Well, God be thanked, as I was sayin', I'm no Pelagian yet.
Now, I'll tak' on ...
    'Morrn, Ferguson. Man, have ye ever thought
What your good leddy costs in coal? ... I'll burn 'em down to
    port.

The Secret of the Machines
(Modern Machinery)

We were taken from the ore-bed and the mine,
   We were melted in the furnace and the pit –
We were cast and wrought and hammered to design,
   We were cut and filed and tooled and gauged to fit.
Some water, coal, and oil is all we ask,
   And a thousandth of an inch to give us play:
And now, if you will set us to our task,
   We will serve you four and twenty hours a day!

     We can pull and haul and push and lift and drive,
     We can print and plough and weave and heat and light,
     We can run and race and swim and fly and dive,
     We can see and hear and count and read and write!

Would you call a friend from half across the world?
   If you'll let us have his name and town and state,
You shall see and hear your crackling question hurled
   Across the arch of heaven while you wait.
Has he answered? Does he need you at his side?
   You can start this very evening if you choose,
And take the Western Ocean in the stride
   Of seventy thousand horses and some screws!

The boat express is waiting your command!
You will find the *Mauretania* at the quay,
Till her captain turns the lever 'neath his hand,
And the monstrous nine-decked city goes to sea.

Do you wish to make the mountains bare their head
And lay their new-cut forests at your feet?
Do you want to turn a river in its bed,
Or plant a barren wilderness with wheat?
Shall we pipe aloft and bring you water down
From the never-failing cisterns of the snows,
To work the mills and tramways in your town,
And irrigate your orchards as it flows?

It is easy! Give us dynamite and drills!
Watch the iron-shouldered rocks lie down and quake,
As the thirsty desert-level floods and fills,
And the valley we have dammed becomes a lake.

But remember, please, the Law by which we live,
    We are not built to comprehend a lie,
We can neither love nor pity nor forgive.
    If you make a slip in handling us you die!
We are greater than the Peoples or the Kings –
    Be humble, as you crawl beneath our rods! –
Our touch can alter all created things,
    We are everything on earth – except The Gods!

Though our smoke may hide the Heavens from your eyes,
    It will vanish and the stars will shine again,
Because, for all our power and weight and size,
    We are nothing more than children of your brain!

Recessional
(1897)

God of our fathers, known of old,
Lord of our far-flung battle line,
Beneath whose awful Hand we hold
Dominion over palm and pine –
Lord God of Hosts, be with us yet,
Lest we forget – lest we forget!

The tumult and the shouting dies;
The Captains and the Kings depart:
Still stands Thine ancient sacrifice,
An humble and a contrite heart.
Lord God of Hosts, be with us yet,
Lest we forget – lest we forget!

Far-called, our navies melt away;
On dune and headland sinks the fire:
Lo, all our pomp of yesterday
Is one with Nineveh and Tyre!
Judge of the Nations, spare us yet,
Lest we forget – lest we forget!

If, drunk with sight of power, we loose
Wild tongues that have not Thee in awe,
Such boastings as the Gentiles use,
Or lesser breeds without the Law –
Lord God of Hosts, be with us yet,
Lest we forget – lest we forget!

For heathen heart that puts her trust
In reeking tube and iron shard,
All valiant dust that builds on dust,
And guarding, calls not Thee to guard,
For frantic boast and foolish word,
Thy mercy on Thy People, Lord!

Boots
(Infantry Columns)

We're foot – slog – slog – slog – sloggin' over Africa –
Foot – foot – foot – foot – sloggin' over Africa –
(Boots – boots – boots – boots – movin' up an' down again!)
    There's no discharge in the war!

Seven – six – eleven – five – nine-an'-twenty mile to-day –
Four – eleven – seventeen – thirty-two the day before –
(Boots – boots – boots – boots – movin' up an' down again!)
    There's no discharge in the war!

Don't – don't – don't – don't – look at what's in front of you.
(Boots – boots – boots – boots – movin' up an' down again);
Men – men – men – men – men go mad with watchin' 'em,
    An' there's no discharge in the war!

Try – try – try – try – to think o' something different –
Oh – my – God – keep – me from goin' lunatic!
(Boots – boots – boots – boots – movin' up an' down again!)
    There's no discharge in the war!

Count – count – count – count – the bullets in the bandoliers.
If – your – eyes – drop – they will get atop o' you!
(Boots – boots – boots – boots – movin' up an' down again) –
　　　　　There's no discharge in the war!

We – can – stick – out – 'unger, thirst, an' weariness,
But – not – not – not – not the chronic sight of 'em –
Boots – boots – boots – boots – movin' up an' down again,
　　　　　An' there's no discharge in the war!

'Tain't – so – bad – by – day because o' company,
But night – brings – long – strings – o' forty thousand million
Boots – boots – boots – boots – movin' up an' down again.
　　　　　There's no discharge in the war!

I – 'ave – marched – six – weeks in 'Ell an' certify
It – is – not – fire – devils, dark, or anything,
But boots – boots – boots – boots – movin' up an' down again,
　　　　　An' there's no discharge in the war!

Arithmetic on the Frontier

A great and glorious thing it is
  To learn, for seven years or so,
The Lord knows what of that and this,
  Ere reckoned fit to face the foe –
The flying bullet down the Pass,
That whistles clear: 'All flesh is grass.'

Three hundred pounds per annum spent
  On making brain and body meeter
For all the murderous intent
  Comprised in 'villainous saltpetre'!
And after – ask the Yusufzaies
What comes of all our 'ologies.

A scrimmage in a Border Station –
  A canter down some dark defile –
Two thousand pounds of education
  Drops to a ten-rupee *jezail*[1] –
The Crammer's boast, the Squadron's pride,
Shot like a rabbit in a ride!

No proposition Euclid wrote,
  No formulae the text-books know,
Will turn the bullet from your coat,
  Or ward the *tulwar*'s[2] downward blow
Strike hard who cares – shoot straight who can –
The odds are on the cheaper man.

One sword-knot stolen from the camp
  Will pay for all the school expenses
Of any Kurrum Valley scamp
  Who knows no word of moods and tenses,
But, being blessed with perfect sight,
Picks off our messmates left and right.

With home-bred hordes the hillsides teem,
  The troop-ships bring us one by one,
At vast expense of time and steam,
  To slay Afridis where they run.
The 'captives of our bow and spear'
Are cheap, alas! as we are dear.

[1] cheap, native musket

[2] sword

Ford o' Kabul River

Kabul town's by Kabul river –
Blow the bugle, draw the sword –
There I lef' my mate for ever,
Wet an' drippin' by the ford.
   Ford, ford, ford o' Kabul river,
   Ford o' Kabul river in the dark!
   There's the river up and brimmin', an' there's 'arf a squadron
     swimmin'
   'Cross the ford o' Kabul river in the dark.

Kabul town's a blasted place –
Blow the bugle, draw the sword –
'Strewth I sha'n't forget 'is face
Wet an' drippin' by the ford!
   Ford, ford, ford o' Kabul river,
   Ford o' Kabul river in the dark!
   Keep the crossing-stakes beside you, an' they will surely guide
     you
   'Cross the ford o' Kabul river in the dark.

Kabul town is sun and dust –
Blow the bugle, draw the sword –
I'd ha' sooner drownded fust
'Stead of 'im beside the ford!
  Ford, ford, ford o' Kabul river,
  Ford o' Kabul river in the dark!
  You can 'ear the 'orses threshin', you can 'ear the men
    a-splashin',
  'Cross the ford o' Kabul river in the dark.

Kabul town was ours to take –
Blow the bugle, draw the sword –
I'd ha' left it for 'is sake –
'Im that left me by the ford.
  Ford, ford, ford o' Kabul river,
  Ford o' Kabul river in the dark!
  It's none so bloomin' dry there; ain't you never comin' nigh
    there,
  'Cross the ford o' Kabul river in the dark?

Kabul town'll go to hell –
Blow the bugle, draw the sword –
'Fore I see him 'live an' well –
'Im the best beside the ford.
   Ford, ford, ford o' Kabul river,
   Ford o' Kabul river in the dark!
   Gawd 'elp 'em if they blunder, for their boots'll pull 'em under,
   By the ford o' Kabul river in the dark.

Turn your 'orse from Kabul town –
Blow the bugle, draw the sword –
'Im an' 'arf my troop is down,
Down an' drownded by the ford.
   Ford, ford, ford o' Kabul river,
   Ford o' Kabul river in the dark!
   There's the river low an' fallin', but it ain't no use a-callin'
   'Cross the ford o' Kabul river in the dark.

The Young British Soldier

When the 'arf-made recruity goes out to the East
'E acts like a babe an' 'e drinks like a beast,
An' 'e wonders because 'e is frequent deceased
Ere 'e's fit for to serve as a soldier.
   Serve, serve, serve as a soldier,
   Serve, serve, serve as a soldier,
   Serve, serve, serve as a soldier,
   So-oldier *of* the Queen!

Now all you recruities what's drafted to-day,
You shut up your rag-box an' 'ark to my lay,
An' I'll sing you a soldier as far as I may:
A soldier what's fit for a soldier.
   Fit, fit, fit for a soldier . . .

First mind you steer clear o' the grog-sellers' huts,
For they sell you Fixed Bay'nets that rots out your guts –
Ay, drink that 'ud eat the live steel from your butts –
An' it's bad for the young British soldier.
   Bad, bad, bad for the soldier . . .

When the cholera comes – as it will past a doubt –
Keep out of the wet and don't go on the shout,
For the sickness gets in as the liquor dies out,
An' it crumples the young British soldier.
    Crum-, crum-, crumples the soldier . . .

But the worst o' your foes is the sun over'ead:
You *must* wear your 'elmet for all that is said:
If 'e finds you uncovered 'e'll knock you down dead,
An' you'll die like a fool of a soldier.
    Fool, fool, fool of a soldier . . .

If you're cast for fatigue by a sergeant unkind,
Don't grouse like a woman nor crack on nor blind;
Be handy and civil, and then you will find
That it's beer for the young British soldier.
    Beer, beer, beer for the soldier . . .

Now, if you must marry, take care she is old –
A troop-sergeant's widow's the nicest, I'm told,
For beauty won't help if your rations is cold,
Nor love ain't enough for a soldier.
    'Nough, 'nough, 'nough for a soldier . . .

If the wife should go wrong with a comrade, be loath
To shoot when you catch 'em – you'll swing, on my oath! –
Make 'im take 'er and keep 'er: that's Hell for them both,
An' you're shut o' the curse of a soldier.
    Curse, curse, curse of a soldier . . .

When first under fire an' you're wishful to duck,
Don't look nor take 'eed at the man that is struck,
Be thankful you're livin', and trust to your luck
And march to your front like a soldier.
    Front, front, front like a soldier . . .

When 'arf of your bullets fly wide in the ditch,
Don't call your Martini a cross-eyed old bitch;
She's human as you are – you treat her as sich,
An' she'll fight for the young British soldier.
    Fight, fight, fight for the soldier . . .

When shakin' their bustles like ladies so fine,
The guns o' the enemy wheel into line,
Shoot low at the limbers an' don't mind the shine,
For noise never startles the soldier.
    Start-, start-, startles the soldier . . .

If your officer's dead and the sergeants look white,
Remember it's ruin to run from a fight:
So take open order, lie down, and sit tight,
And wait for supports like a soldier.
  Wait, wait, wait like a soldier . . .

When you're wounded and left on Afghanistan's plains,
And the women come out to cut up what remains,
Jest roll to your rifle and blow out your brains
An' go to your Gawd like a soldier.
  Go, go, go like a soldier,
  Go, go, go like a soldier,
  Go, go, go like a soldier,
  So-oldier *of* the Queen!

Gentlemen-Rankers

To the legion of the lost ones, to the cohort of the damned,
    To my brethren in their sorrow overseas,
Sings a gentleman of England cleanly bred, machinely crammed,
    And a trooper of the Empress, if you please.
Yea, a trooper of the forces who has run his own six horses,
    And faith he went the pace and went it blind,
And the world was more than kin while he held the ready tin,
    But to-day the Sergeant's something less than kind.
      We're poor little lambs who've lost our way,
        Baa! Baa! Baa!
      We're little black sheep who've gone astray,
        Baa–aa–aa!
      Gentlemen-rankers out on the spree,
      Damned from here to Eternity,
      God ha' mercy on such as we,
        Baa! Yah! Bah!

Oh, it's sweet to sweat through stables, sweet to empty kitchen
    slops,
    And it's sweet to hear the tales the troopers tell,
To dance with blowzy housemaids at the regimental hops
    And thrash the cad who says you waltz too well.

Yes, it makes you cock-a-hoop to be 'Rider' to your troop,
    And branded with a blasted worsted spur,
When you envy, O how keenly, one poor Tommy living cleanly
    Who blacks your boots and sometimes calls you 'Sir'.

If the home we never write to, and the oaths we never keep,
    And all we know most distant and most dear,
Across the snoring barrack-room return to break our sleep,
    Can you blame us if we soak ourselves in beer?
When the drunken comrade mutters and the great guard-lantern
    gutters
    And the horror of our fall is written plain,
Every secret, self-revealing on the aching whitewashed ceiling,
    Do you wonder that we drug ourselves from pain?

We have done with Hope and Honour, we are lost to Love and
    Truth,
    We are dropping down the ladder rung by rung,
And the measure of our torment is the measure of our youth.
    God help us, for we knew the worst too young!
Our shame is clean repentance for the crime that brought the
    sentence,
    Our pride it is to know no spur of pride,
And the Curse of Reuben holds us till an alien turf enfolds us
    And we die, and none can tell Them where we died.

We're poor little lambs who've lost our way,
  Baa! Baa! Baa!
We're little black sheep who've gone astray,
  Baa–aa–aa!
Gentlemen-rankers out on the spree,
Damned from here to Eternity,
God ha' mercy on such as we,
  Baa! Yah! Bah!

A Smuggler's Song

('Hal o' the Draft', *Puck of Pook's Hill*, 1906)

If you wake at midnight, and hear a horse's feet,
Don't go drawing back the blind, or looking in the street.
Them that ask no questions isn't told a lie.
Watch the wall, my darling, while the Gentlemen go by!
   Five and twenty ponies,
   Trotting through the dark –
   Brandy for the Parson,
   'Baccy for the Clerk;
   Laces for a lady, letters for a spy,
And watch the wall, my darling, while the Gentlemen go by!

Running round the woodlump if you chance to find
Little barrels, roped and tarred, all full of brandy-wine,
Don't you shout to come and look, nor use 'em for your play.
Put the brishwood back again – and they'll be gone next day!

If you see the stable-door setting open wide;
If you see a tired horse lying down inside;
If your mother mends a coat cut about and tore;
If the lining's wet and warm – don't you ask no more!

If you meet King George's men, dressed in blue and red,
You be carefull what you say, and mindful what is said.
If they call you 'pretty maid', and chuck you 'neath the chin,
Don't you tell where no one is, nor yet where no one's been!

Knocks and footsteps round the house – whistles after dark –
You've no call for running out till the house-dogs bark.
Trusty's here, and *Pincher's* here, and see how dumb they lie –
They don't fret to follow when the Gentlemen go by!

If you do as you've been told, 'likely there's a chance,
You'll be given a dainty doll, all the way from France,
With a cap of Valenciennes, and a velvet hood –
A present from the Gentlemen, along o' being good!
    Five and twenty ponies,
    Trotting through the dark –
    Brandy for the Parson,
    'Baccy for the Clerk;
Them that asks no questions isn't told a lie –
Watch the wall, my darling, while the Gentlemen go by!

Jane's Marriage

('The Janeites', *Debits and Credits*, 1924)

Jane went to Paradise:
   That was only fair.
Good Sir Walter met her first,
   And led her up the stair.
Henry and Tobias,
   And Miguel of Spain,
Stood with Shakespeare at the top
   To welcome Jane –

Then the Three Archangels
   Offered out of hand,
Anything in Heaven's gift
   That she might command.
Azrael's eyes upon her,
   Raphael's wings above,
Michael's sword against her heart,
   Jane said: 'Love.'

Instantly the under-
   standing Seraphim
Laid their fingers on their lips
   And went to look for him.

Stole across the Zodiac,
  Harnessed Charles's Wain,
And whispered round the Nebulae
  'Who loved Jane?'

In a private limbo
  Where none had thought to look,
Sat a Hampshire gentleman
  Reading of a book.
It was called *Persuasion*,
  And it told the plain
Story of the love between
  Him and Jane.

He heard the question
  Circle Heaven through –
Closed the book and answered:
  'I did – and do!'
Quietly but speedily
  (As Captain Wentworth moved)
Entered into Paradise
  The man Jane loved!

If—

('Brother Square-Toes', *Rewards and Fairies*, 1910)

If you can keep your head when all about you
Are losing theirs and blaming it on you;
If you can trust yourself when all men doubt you,
But make allowance for their doubting too;
If you can wait and not be tired by waiting,
Or, being lied about, don't deal in lies,
Or being hated, don't give way to hating,
And yet don't look too good, nor talk too wise;

If you can dream – and not make dreams your master;
If you can think – and not make thoughts your aim;
If you can meet with Triumph and Disaster
And treat those two impostors just the same;
If you can bear to hear the truth you've spoken
Twisted by knaves to make a trap for fools,
Or watch the things you gave your life to, broken,
And stoop and build 'em up with worn-out tools:

If you can make one heap of all your winnings
And risk it on one turn of pitch-and-toss,
And lose, and start again at your beginnings,
And never breathe a word about your loss;
If you can force your heart and nerve and sinew
To serve your turn long after they are gone,
And so hold on when there is nothing in you
Except the Will which says to them: 'Hold on!'

If you can talk with crowds and keep your virtue,
Or walk with Kings – nor lose the common touch,
If neither foes nor loving friends can hurt you,
If all men count with you, but none too much;
If you can fill the unforgiving minute
With sixty seconds' worth of distance run,
Yours is the Earth and everything that's in it,
And – which is more – you'll be a Man, my son!

The Female of the Species
(a response to the Suffragist movement, 1911)

When the Himalayan peasant meets the he-bear in his pride,
He shouts to scare the monster, who will often turn aside.
But the she-bear thus accosted rends the peasant tooth and nail.
For the female of the species is more deadly than the male.

When Nag the basking cobra hears the careless foot of man,
He will sometimes wriggle sideways and avoid it if he can.
But his mate makes no such motion where she camps beside the
    trail.
For the female of the species is more deadly than the male.

When the early Jesuit fathers preached to Hurons and Choctaws,
They prayed to be delivered from the vengeance of the squaws.
'Twas the women, not the warriors, turned those stark enthusiasts
    pale.
For the female of the species is more deadly than the male.

Man's timid heart is bursting with the things he must not say,
For the Woman that God gave him isn't his to give away;
But when hunter meets with husbands, each confirms the
  other's tale –
The female of the species is more deadly than the male.

Man, a bear in most relations – worm and savage otherwise, –
Man propounds negotiations, Man accepts the compromise.
Very rarely will he squarely push the logic of a fact
To its ultimate conclusion in unmitigated act.

Fear, or foolishness, impels him, ere he lay the wicked low,
To concede some form of trial even to his fiercest foe.
Mirth obscene diverts his anger – Doubt and Pity oft perplex
Him in dealing with an issue – to the scandal of The Sex!

But the Woman that God gave him, every fibre of her frame
Proves her launched for one sole issue, armed and engined for
  the same,
And to serve that single issue, lest the generations fail,
The female of the species must be deadlier than the male.

She who faces Death by torture for each life beneath her breast
May not deal in doubt or pity – must not swerve for fact or jest.
These be purely male diversions – not in these her honour
    dwells.
She the Other Law we live by, is that Law and nothing else.

She can bring no more to living than the powers that make her
    great
As the Mother of the Infant and the Mistress of the Mate.
And when Babe and Man are lacking and she strides unchained
    to claim
Her right as femme (and baron), her equipment is the same.

She is wedded to convictions – in default of grosser ties;
Her contentions are her children, Heaven help him who denies! –
He will meet no suave discussion, but the instant, white-hot, wild,
Wakened female of the species warring as for spouse and child.

Unprovoked and awful charges – even so the she-bear fights,
Speech that drips, corrodes, and poisons – even so the cobra
    bites,
Scientific vivisection of one nerve till it is raw
And the victim writhes in anguish – like the Jesuit with the
    squaw!

So it comes that Man, the coward, when he gathers to confer
With his fellow-braves in council, dare not leave a place for her
Where, at war with Life and Conscience, he uplifts his erring
    hands
To some God of Abstract Justice – which no woman understands.

And Man knows it! Knows, moreover, that the Woman that God
    gave him
Must command but may not govern – shall enthral but not
    enslave him.
And *She* knows, because She warns him, and Her instincts never
    fail,
That the Female of Her Species is more deadly than the Male.

The Nursing Sister

(Maternity Hospital)

(from *The Naulahka*, 1892)

Our sister sayeth such and such,
And we must bow to her behests.
Our sister toileth overmuch,
Our little maid that hath no breasts.

A field untilled, a web unwove,
A flower withheld from sun or bee,
An alien in the Courts of Love,
And – teacher unto such as we!

We love her, but we laugh the while,
We laugh, but sobs are mixed with laughter;
Our sister hath no time to smile,
She knows not what must follow after.

Wind of the South, arise and blow,
From beds of spice thy locks shake free;
Breathe on her heart that she may know,
Breathe on her eyes that she may see!

Alas! we vex her with our mirth,
And maze her with most tender scorn,
Who stands beside the Gates of Birth,
Herself a child – a child unborn!

Our sister sayeth such and such,
And we must bow to her behests.
Our sister toileth overmuch,
Our little maid that hath no breasts.

The Dirge of Dead Sisters
1902
(For the Nurses who died in the South African War)

Who recalls the twilight and the rangèd tents in order
(Violet peaks uplifted through the crystal evening air?)
And clink of iron teacups and the piteous, noble laughter,
And the faces of the Sisters with the dust upon their hair?

(Now and not hereafter, while the breath is in our nostrils,
Now and not hereafter, ere the meaner years go by –
Let us now remember many honourable women,
Such as bade us turn again when we were like to die.)

Who recalls the morning and the thunder through the foothills,
(Tufts of fleecy shrapnel strung along the empty plains?)
And the sun-scarred Red-Cross coaches creeping guarded to the
    culvert,
And the faces of the Sisters looking gravely from the trains?

(When the days were torment and the nights were clouded terror,
When the Powers of Darkness had dominion on our soul –
When we fled consuming through the Seven Hells of Fever,
These put out their hands to us and healed and made us whole.)

Who recalls the midnight by the bridge's wrecked abutment,
(Autumn rain that rattled like a Maxim on the tin?)
And the lightning-dazzled levels and the streaming, straining
    wagons,
And the faces of the Sisters as they bore the wounded in?

(Till the pain was merciful and stunned us into silence –
When each nerve cried out on God that made the misused clay;
When the Body triumphed and the last poor shame departed –
These abode our agonies and wiped the sweat away.)

Who recalls the noontide and the funerals through the market,
(Blanket-hidden bodies, flagless, followed by the flies?)
And the footsore firing-party, and the dust and stench and
    staleness,
And the faces of the Sisters and the glory in their eyes?

(Bold behind the battle, in the open camp all-hallowed,
Patient, wise, and mirthful in the ringed and reeking town,
These endured unresting till they rested from their labours –
Little wasted bodies, ah, so light to lower down!)

Yet their graves are scattered and their names are clean forgotten,
Earth shall not remember, but the Waiting Angel knows
Them that died at Uitvlugt when the plague was on the city –
Her that fell at Simon's Town[1] in service on our foes.

Wherefore we they ransomed, while the breath is in our
    nostrils,
Now and not hereafter – ere the meaner years go by –
Praise with love and worship many honourable women,
Those that gave their lives for us when we were like to die!

[1] Mary Kingsley

The Absent-Minded Beggar
(1899)

When you've shouted 'Rule Britannia', when you've sung 'God
    save the Queen' –
  When you've finished killing Kruger with your mouth,
Will you kindly drop a shilling in my little tambourine
  For a gentleman in khaki ordered South?
He's an absent-minded beggar, and his weaknesses are great –
  But we and Paul[1] must take him as we find him –
He is out on active service, wiping something off a slate –
  And he's left a lot of little things behind him!
Duke's son – cook's son – son of a hundred kings –
  (Fifty thousand horse and foot going to Table Bay!)
Each of 'em doing his country's work
  (and who's to look after their things?)
Pass the hat for your credit's sake,
                and pay – pay – pay!

[1] Paul Kruger, President of the Transvaal

There are girls he married secret, asking no permission to,
    For he knew he wouldn't get it if he did.
There is gas and coals and vittles, and the house-rent falling due,
    And it's more than rather likely there's a kid.
There are girls he walked with casual. They'll be sorry now he's
      gone,
    For an absent-minded beggar they will find him,
But it ain't the time for sermons with the winter coming on –
    We must help the girl that Tommy's left behind him!
Cook's son – Duke's son – son of a belted Earl –
    Son of a Lambeth publican – it's all the same to-day!
Each of 'em doing his country's work
    (and who's to look after the girl?)
Pass the hat for your credit's sake,

                and pay – pay – pay!

There are families by thousands, far too proud to beg or speak,
    And they'll put their sticks and bedding up the spout,
And they'll live on half o' nothing, paid 'em punctual once a
    week,
    'Cause the man that earns the wage is ordered out.
He's an absent-minded beggar, but he heard his country call,
    And his reg'ment didn't need to send to find him!
He chucked his job and joined it – so the job before us all
    Is to help the home that Tommy's left behind him!
Duke's job – cook's job – gardener, baronet, groom,
    Mews or palace or paper-shop – there's someone gone away!
Each of 'em doing his country's work
    (and who's to look after the room?)
Pass the hat for your credit's sake,
                            and pay – pay – pay!

Let us manage so as, later, we can look him in the face,
    And tell him – what he'd very much prefer –
That, while he saved the Empire, his employer saved his place,
    And his mates (that's you and me) looked out for *her*.
He's an absent-minded beggar and he may forget it all,
    But we do not want his kiddies to remind him,
That we sent 'em to the workhouse while their daddy hammered
    Paul,
    So we'll help the homes that Tommy left behind him!
Cook's home – Duke's home – home of a millionaire,
    (Fifty thousand horse and foot going to Table Bay!)
Each of 'em doing his country's work
    (and what have you got to spare?)
Pass the hat for your credit's sake,
                    and pay – pay – pay!

The Way Through the Woods

('Marklake Witches', *Rewards and Fairies*, 1910)

They shut the road through the woods
Seventy years ago.
Weather and rain have undone it again,
And now you would never know
There was once a road through the woods
Before they planted the trees.
It is underneath the coppice and heath,
And the thin anemones.
Only the keeper sees
That, where the ring-dove broods,
And the badgers roll at ease,
There was once a road through the woods.

Yet, if you enter the woods
Of a summer evening late,
When the night-air cools on the trout-ringed pools
Where the otter whistles his mate,
(They fear not men in the woods,
Because they see so few)
You will hear the beat of a horse's feet,
And the swish of a skirt in the dew,
Steadily cantering through
The misty solitudes,
As though they perfectly knew
The old lost road through the woods . . .
But there is no road through the woods.

For All We Have and Are
1914

For all we have and are,
For all our children's fate,
Stand up and take the war.
The Hun is at the gate!
Our world has passed away
In wantonness o'erthrown.
There is nothing left to-day
But steel and fire and stone!
   Though all we knew depart,
    The old Commandments stand: –
    'In courage keep your heart,
    In strength lift up your hand.'

Once more we hear the word
That sickened earth of old: –
'No law except the Sword
Unsheathed and uncontrolled.'
Once more it knits mankind,
Once more the nations go
To meet and break and bind
A crazed and driven foe.

Comfort, content, delight,
The ages' slow-bought gain,
They shrivelled in a night.
Only ourselves remain
To face the naked days
In silent fortitude,
Through perils and dismays
Renewed and re-renewed.
    Though all we made depart,
    The old Commandments stand: –
    'In patience keep your heart,
    In strength lift up your hand.'

No easy hope or lies
Shall bring us to our goal,
But iron sacrifice
Of body, will, and soul.
There is but one task for all –
One life for each to give.
What stands if Freedom fall?
Who dies if England live?

Mine Sweepers
1914–18
(Sea Warfare)

Dawn off the Foreland – the young flood making
Jumbled and short and steep –
Black in the hollows and bright where it's breaking –
Awkward water to sweep.
'Mines reported in the fairway,
Warn all traffic and detain.
'Sent up *Unity*, *Claribel*, *Assyrian*, *Stormcock*, and
   Golden Gain.'

Noon off the Foreland – the first ebb making
Lumpy and strong in the bight.
Boom after boom, and the golf-hut shaking
And the jackdaws wild with fright!
'Mines located in the fairway,
Boats now working up the chain,
Sweepers – *Unity*, *Claribel*, *Assyrian*, *Stormcock*, and
   Golden Gain.'

Dusk off the Foreland – the last light going
And the traffic crowding through,
And five damned trawlers with their syreens blowing
Heading the whole review!
'Sweep completed in the fairway.
No more mines remain.
'Sent back *Unity*, *Claribel*, *Assyrian*, *Stormcock*, and
Golden Gain.'

Mesopotamia
1917

They shall not return to us, the resolute, the young,
The eager and whole-hearted whom we gave:
But the men who left them thriftily to die in their own dung,
Shall they come with years and honour to the grave?

They shall not return to us, the strong men coldly slain
In sight of help denied from day to day:
But the men who edged their agonies and chid them in their pain,
Are they too strong and wise to put away?

Our dead shall not return to us while Day and Night divide –
Never while the bars of sunset hold.
But the idle-minded overlings who quibbled while they died,
Shall they thrust for high employments as of old?

Shall we only threaten and be angry for an hour?
When the storm is ended shall we find
How softly but how swiftly they have sidled back to power
By the favour and contrivance of their kind?

Even while they soothe us, while they promise large amends,
Even while they make a show of fear,
Do they call upon their debtors, and take counsel with their
    friends,
To confirm and re-establish each career?

Their lives cannot repay us – their death could not undo –
The shame that they have laid upon our race.
But the slothfulness that wasted and the arrogance that slew,
Shell we leave it unabated in its place?

Gethsemane
(1914–18)

The Garden called Gethsemane
In Picardy it was,
And there the people came to see
The English soldiers pass.
We used to pass – we used to pass
Or halt, as it might be,
And ship our masks in case of gas
Beyond Gethsemane.

The Garden called Gethsemane,
It held a pretty lass,
But all the time she talked to me
I prayed my cup might pass.
The officer sat in the chair,
The men lay on the grass,
And all the time we halted there
I prayed my cup might pass.

It didn't pass – it didn't pass –
It didn't pass from me.
I drank it when we met the gas
Beyond Gethsemane!

From 'Epitaphs of the War':
1914–18

Batteries out of ammunition

If any mourn us in the workshop, say
We died because the shift kept holiday.

A drifter off Tarentum

He from the wind-bitten north with ship and companions
   descended,
Searching for eggs of death spawned by invisible hulls.
Many he found and drew forth. Of a sudden the fishery ended
In flame and a clamorous breath known to the eye-pecking gulls.

The coward

I could not look on Death, which being known,
Men led me to him, blindfold and alone.

The beginner

On the first hour of my first day
In the front trench I fell.
(Children in boxes at a play
Stand up to watch it well.)

A son

My son was killed while laughing at some jest. I would I knew
What it was, and it might serve me in a time when jests are few.

'Equality of sacrifice'

A. 'I was a "Have".' B. 'I was a "Have-not".'
(*Together*) 'What hast thou given which I gave not?'

The refined man

I was of delicate mind. I stepped aside for my needs,
Disdaining the common office. I was seen from afar and
  killed . . .
How is this matter for mirth? Let each man be judged by his deeds.
I have paid my price to live with myself on the terms that I
  willed.

Common form

If any question why we died,
Tell them, because our fathers lied.

Hindu Sepoy in France

This man in his own country prayed we know not to what Powers.
We pray Them to reward him for his bravery in ours.

My Boy Jack
1914–18

'Have you news of my boy Jack?'
Not this tide.
'When d'you think that he'll come back?'
Not with this wind blowing, and this tide.

'Has any one else had word of him?'
Not this tide.
For what is sunk will hardly swim,
Not with this wind blowing, and this tide.

'Oh, dear, what comfort can I find?'
None this tide,
Nor any tide,
Except he did not shame his kind –
 Not even with that wind blowing, and that tide.

Then hold your head up all the more,
This tide,
And every tide;
Because he was the son you bore,
And gave to that wind blowing and that tide!

The Children
1914–18
('The Honours of War', *A Diversity of Creatures*, 1917)

These were our children who died for our lands: they were dear
    in our sight.
  We have only the memory left of their home-treasured sayings
    and laughter.
  The price of our loss shall be paid to our hands, not another's
    hereafter.
Neither the Alien nor Priest shall decide on it. That is our right.
  But who shall return us the children?

At the hour the Barbarian chose to disclose his pretences,
  And raged against Man, they engaged, on the breasts that they
    bared for us,
  The first felon-stroke of the sword he had long-time prepared
    for us –
Their bodies were all our defence while we wrought our defences.

They bought us anew with their blood, forbearing to blame us,
Those hours which we had not made good when the Judgment
    o'ercame us.

They believed us and perished for it. Our statecraft, our learning
Delivered them bound to the Pit and alive to the burning
Whither they mirthfully hastened as jostling for honour –
Not since her birth has our Earth seen such worth loosed upon
     her.

Nor was their agony brief, or once only imposed on them.
  The wounded, the war-spent, the sick received no exemption:
  Being cured they returned and endured and achieved our
     redemption,
Hopeless themselves of relief, till Death, marvelling, closed on
     them.

That flesh we had nursed from the first in all cleanness was given
To corruption unveiled and assailed by the malice of Heaven –
By the heart-shaking jests of Decay where it lolled on the wires –
To be blanched or gay-painted by fumes – to be cindered by
     fires –
To be senselessly tossed and retossed in stale mutilation
From crater to crater. For this we shall take expiation.
  But who shall return us our children?

Sepulchral
(FROM THE GREEK ANTHOLOGIES)

Swifter than aught 'neath the sun the car of Simonides
   moved him.
Two things he could not out-run – Death and a Woman who
   loved him.

The Tour
(BYRON)

Thirteen as twelve my Murray always took –
He was a publisher. The new Police
Have neater ways of bringing men to book,
So Juan found himself before J.P.'s .
Accused of storming through that placid nook
At practically any pace you please.
The Dogberry, and the Waterbury, made
It fifty mile – five pounds. And Juan paid!

The Idiot Boy

(WORDSWORTH)

He wandered down the mountain grade
Beyond the speed assigned –
A youth whom Justice often stayed
And generally fined.

He went alone, that none might know
If he could drive or steer.
Now he is in the ditch, and Oh!
The differential gear!

The Braggart

(MAT. PRIOR)

Petrolio, vaunting his Mercedes' power,
Vows she can cover eighty miles an hour.
I tried the car of old and know she can.
But dare he ever wake her? Ask his man!

The Storm Cone
1932

This is the midnight – let no star
Delude us – dawn is very far.
This is the tempest long foretold –
Slow to make head but sure to hold.

Stand by! The lull 'twixt blast and blast
Signals the storm is near, not past;
And worse than present jeopardy
May our forlorn tomorrow be.

If we have cleared the expectant reef,
Let no man look for his relief.
Only the darkness holds the shape
Of further peril to escape.

It is decreed that we abide
The weight of gale against the tide
And those huge waves the outer main
Sends in to set us back again.

They fall and whelm. We strive to hear
The pulses of her labouring gear,
Till the deep throb beneath us proves,
After each shudder and check, she moves!

She moves, with all save purpose lost,
To make her offing from the coast;
But, till she fetches open sea,
Let no man deem that he is free!

INDEX OF FIRST LINES